Do People Look Up at the Moon Anymore?

Do People Look Up
at the Moon Anymore?

O

Poems

For Therese & Tom
best wishes always

1 2015

Robert A Rosenstone

Sharq Press
Pacific Palisades, California

Sharq Press
Pacific Palisades, California
www.sharqart.com
www.rosenstone.com

ISBN: 9-780-69239-950-7

Cover and author photographs by Nahid Massoud

for N

always

Table of Contents

Way Back When

↻

Do people look up at the moon anymore?

Do people look up at the moon anymore?
It's hard to find the time these days
what with all the tweeting and twattering
not to mention the visits to doctor's offices
where parking costs more than a specialist did
way back when I was a kid.
Looking at the moon is for young lovers,
at least it was *in my day*
(a phrase I never thought I'd ever use way back when).
Maybe they look at the moon on that app now,
Night Sky, I think it's called.
Plato may have been right about the way
we spend our lives staring
at shadows on a wall.
But it's getting to feel a lot less like living a cave
and more like a matrix,
though I couldn't sit through the film,
not with those cheesy sets,
cardboard or cgi
disguised by a lot of clanking and rumbling
produced by foley guys,
who may well be women.
I understand. I live in this age,
but not for love of it.
The whole thing just seems smaller
than way back when.
Our world had real Nazis,
Hitler, Himmler, Heydrich,
not actors with German accents.

I doubt my father ever looked at the moon
with or without my Mom.
More likely he gave or took odds
on how long it would take to come out
from behind that cloud, five minutes or fifteen.
When we looked at the moon
way back when,
it promised something we could never name
but we knew it would be Huge.
Now everyone keeps saying the world is smaller,
the globe has shrunk. Then along comes a smart ass
astronomer (just last week) to tell us it's not the earth,
but the moon that's flaking away.
A few million millennia and nobody will understand
the lyrics of all those pop songs of the forties,
nothing left to rhyme with June and spoon and croon.

So this is what it feels like to be seventy-four

So this is what it feels like to be seventy four.
Who would'a thunk it, as Pogo would have said,
and who would have thunk Charlie Brown's creator
would be such a good Christian.
All those years of God talking to us
through Lucy and Linus and Schroeder.
He must speak every known language
and a whole bunch yet to be invented.
No matter which one you understand
it's difficult to know His intentions,
what He's saying, how He's saying it.
This is no doubt blasphemy
in just about any religion you can name
and lots of those you can't.
But you don't have belong to one
to acknowledge His accomplishments
along with His failures.
My guess is He would fess up to them a lot quicker
than those who claim a direct line to His brain.
As if He needs the organs of mortality!
Imagine the enormous headaches He would get
trying to keep order in this universe
with all its galaxies and dimensions,
tribes, clans, nations, and alliances.
Enough to make him seek another line of work?
Maybe being God isn't all it's cracked up to be.

So this is what it's like to be seventy-four.
Unthunk, unthinkable. Yet here it is.

Days that make you want to write sad poetry
full of the wisdom you claim to have gained
over all these years.
Tell me that isn't a sign of being seventy-four!
Truth is, I know lots of things you say
before you say them,
for I have said them
when I was younger and the world was too.
Tell me: did we all stop caring at once,
or did the passions leak away over the years?
Or was it never more than ego
parading in the name of an ideology
you never could define, but ideology it was,
one third Marx, one third New Age mumbo jumbo,
and one third–hell, at lot more than that –
pussy and the places it was likely to be found.
That was our real revolution.
and our revelation too,
even if it took a princess
half a century later
to slip a few of His words to me.
I must have been one tough nut to crack,
stiff-necked and stiff so many other places
(oh yeah, at this age you wish),
that a soft approach proved more effective.
People have the wrong idea about pussy.
God is everywhere. I do believe that, but
these days He must be wondering what went wrong
after the experiment with the great apes
turned out so well.
Best we can tell He hasn't bothered
with any new species
for quite some time now,

at least none you'd notice.
Viruses, perhaps, but nothing for the naked eye.
Man was a biggie, The Biggie.
He was to take over the planet
and keep it for God's sake.

So this is what it's like to be seventy-four.
You speak your mind but nobody listens.
They probably never did.
The words were always part of something larger.
I never could believe the Sunday school stories about
that ill-tempered Character who appeared
on almost every page of
When the Jewish People Was Young.
We argued over that *was* for an entire year.
I lost. I was nine. The teacher
was a bearded old man
with a number tattooed on his arm.
His image hovered over all those books
I devoured during high school years
before there was the word, Holocaust.
All we knew were concentration camps,
and believe me, they were way beyond words.

So this is what it's like to be seventy-four
(and three months—already!)
You sit in bed at night writing poetry
instead of thinking about pussy.

You reach a point

You reach
a point
where everything
you see
you seem
to have seen
before.

The same movies
the same awards
the same books
even if
the names
of the authors
their gender
and ethnic backgrounds
have changed.

How many
times
have I read
a review
of a book about
the final
first contact
with
the last unknown
tribe
on the globe?

(until the next one
comes along.)

You know
what I'm talking about,
don't you?
What better
metaphor
for the world,
but the question is
why did I want
to make it mine?
Why were
the words
always more
important
than what
they were about?

And while we're
at it, tell me:
can words
be part of
the divine
even if you
don't
believe in divinity?
And if they are
sacred
why are they profaned
every day
everywhere?

Perhaps that's
a sign
that this isn't
the right world
after all.
This is
just
the one
we got into
by mistake,
and then we spend
the rest of
our life
annoyed
that some day
we have to
get out
of it.

At a certain age

At a certain age you stop going
to concerts of New Music,
exhibitions of the latest dematerialized object
or installations in a gallery of what could be
piles of garbage, but it's not clear
for the light is so dim you can't see a thing,
and someone, the curator, says that's the point!
You avoid all poetry readings.
Slams. Raves. Whatever the latest word
for the oldest profession.
You watch the Turner classic movie channel so much
that Robert Osborne seems like family member,
the annoying cousin who keeps showing up to relate
obscure bits of gossip about people you don't care about
even if they are on the screen
going about the business of being glamorous
as if they will live forever.

This is the Time

So we'll no more go a 'roving
  So late into the night
Though the heart be still as loving
  And the moon be still as bright.

You recognize the stanza if you know Byron,
or if you were a reader of sci-fi,
as we learned to call it way back when
you could still find *Thrilling Wonder Stories*
on newsstands, when there were newstands.
That's where I encountered Ray Bradbury's version
of that moon long before *The Martian Chronicles*
became such a famous book.
It was that summer in Plage Laval
when I first understood the difference between
boys and girls is rather neat, after all.
There was a war on, as there usually is.
The war we would always call it,
the real one with Nazis and Japs,
not these half wars we have fought ever since.
Her name is gone, her face, the color of her hair,
the lips I brushed with mine later that night,
the first of many surprises a female would provide
over the next seven decades.
I remember her bright yellow bathing suit,
the waters of the lake a wavy mirror in the August sun,
the gray raft where our thighs touched,
the first time by accident.

Byron was unusual.
His actions followed his words.
Swimming the Hellespont, whatever that is.
Fighting for Greek independence.
Drowning at Missolonghi and having his body
dragged up on the beach and burned on a pyre –
or was that Shelley at Viareggio?
How much does all this stuff I have forgotten
matter in the greater scheme of things,
or even in the lesser where most of us live?

I never did go roving much, night or day.
The closest was on that first trip to Europe in 1958.
Landing in Hamburg on an Israeli freighter
seemed daring at the time.
My first glimpse of a native
is not the SS man of the movies
some corner of my brain feared might still be alive,
but an ancient hooker,
all lipstick, rouge, wrinkles, and orange hair,
leaning against a dockside bar.
I remember thinking: do people pay to sleep
with someone so decrepit?
She was probably no more than forty.
I was six months out of college,
and practically a virgin,
pregnant with the exploits of Hemingway,
a weekend with a big hipped Austrian girl
in a ski cabin of the Alto Adige,
love and death in the afternoon.

I felt danger only once,
on a dark and rainy night

in the hilly back streets of Naples
where it took forever to find the
Ostelli per gioventu.
Proud I was to ask for the youth hostel in Italian,
but none of the natives, dark men in shabby coats,
understood me, and some of their gestures,
arms punching the air, seemed like threats,
but perhaps they were just pointing directions.
Later trips would be full of projects,
meetings, appointments, dinners,
but way back then I could hitch across Europe,
an American flag pinned to my rucksack.
It helped to get rides and sometimes meals
and cigarettes in Italy and Germany.
France was another story, as it always is.

You Get to an Age

You get to an age
when you see your life as the story it is,
or should I say has been?
Joys and pains together now,
happiness, tragedy, triumph, loss,
not much difference between them.
A time when the issue may be God
But you've never known how to talk about Him.
A curious lack in your education.
You always thought was a plus.

In recent years you wonder
about the words you have been spilling
across pages and screens for sixty years.
Your name gets attached to them.
People invite you to other continents
to hear you say them over again,
and they applaud and shake your hand,
but they're not really yours to begin with,
for you're no more than a messenger
unable to understand the messages you bear.

Remember when

Remember when there was no China?
I mean of course
there was China, a huge country,
millions of people with pigtails
men and women both.
That was one of the funny things
about China.
It was different alright,
but nobody cared very much
other than readers of Pearl Buck,
a few folks in the CIA
and some oil men.
They're always up to no good.
Nobody felt threatened by
China's economy,
or wondered what was going on
inside or in front of
The Great Hall of the People,
or cared about its quarrels with
the Philippines, or Japan, or Taiwan
over some rocky island
in the yellow sea.
There was a Great Wall
to keep out the barbarians.
Us, apparently,
or people like us.
Five thousand years of history.
Perhaps the Chinese knew
what they were doing.

I am amazed

I am amazed at how difficult it is
to pay attention to anything these days.
Is it an illusion that we used to do so?
People weren't dying so often then,
not the ones we knew.
Sure we read the newspaper every day.
TV was for those who never graduated high school,
people living in parts of the city and county
as unreal as Baghdad or whatever town it was
where Ali Baba and his thieves hung out.
El Monte. South Central. Whittier.
In high school those were names to reckon with.
That was about the time
of Adlai Stevenson's concession speech
after his second loss to Ike? Or was it the first?
In the newspaper photo he was dabbing at one eye
with a handkerchief.
Too hurt to smile and too old to cry indeed –
or was it the other way around?
Years later we learn this same hero
(I shook his hand at the Beverly Jewish Center
and didn't wash it for three days)
was telling women to forget about careers,
stay home and bake for your hubby.
So don't tell me times haven't changed.
Flat screens. Iphones. Whatever else
Apple is advertising these days.
Who would have thought we'd still be talking
about the problems of the inner city in 2012?

Or not talking, as usual, and not because
the problems have been solved or even addressed.
Who would have thought Barack Obama,
or George Bush for that matter?
It was foggy, our vision.
Not even a vision really,
more like a kind of hope.
We were sure only good stuff would happen to us
despite the uncle who did time in the penitentiary
and the unknown relatives
with funny names like Ziggy and Sasha,
who vanished somewhere in Europe.
After mother took the telephone call,
she turned off the burner on the stove –
no brisket tonight! –
and covered her eyes with one hand.

May 12, 2011

At this age, seventy five,
the only subject left is God,
but who has the words?
Not me!
In the old days
(even older than me),
they used to go on and on
about the glories of creation,
the mountains, the seas, the wondrous redwoods.
Nature! Still there but
a touch run down these days
what with all the oil spills, clear-cut logging,
bombing raids and occasional missile strikes.
Much of the world is a slum,
and more of it will be soon enough.
Can we blame it on Him
(assuming that's the right gender,
though it's a bigger assumption
than I care to make).
No sparrow falls without His knowing,
so why not every bomb as well?
You might say
we have raised passing the buck
to a high art form.
Still, at 75, there it is
waiting for us to come to grips
with finality.
The closer it gets the more mysterious
the show.

Step right up folks!
Twenty five cents to see
inside the tent,
worlds being born and dying.
You won't believe your eyes!
Personally I think it's more
like one of those games of three card Monte
run by a hustler on the fair ground,
like the one we used to pass each day
on the road between
Trout Lake and St. Agathe,
no more than ten, twelve booths
and a Ferris Wheel that was always
breaking down and leaving you worried
that you'd be stuck way up the in sky forever.
No matter how closely you watch
the cards being shuffled,
you never are able to find the Queen
– or King.

Karen: In Memoriam

Karen was a Romanian.
You would know that already
If you had any of those Levantine folk
in your background.
That made her the sister I never had.
We recognized each other,
not in some man woman way,
nothing like that.
Call it tribal. Call it Romanian.
It's a way that doesn't give a damn
if you spell the country
beginning RO or RU or ROU
because spelling isn't the point.
We never spent much time together.
Thanksgivings mostly. Family affairs
without all the emotional baggage
dining with blood relatives entails.
The thing about our ancestors is that
unlike Russian immigrants
who centered their lives around
societies devoted to changing the world,
or our Polish cousins who lingered
in the courtyards of synagogues
chanting the words of God,
Romanians in America
opened restaurants and night clubs.
You may think this means they made
a business out of pleasure,
but they didn't distinguish between the two.

Karen was their descendant,
no doubt about it.
You might say she made a night club
out of all her days,
but that would be an exaggeration.
Her greatest gift did not
come from tradition,
but from that self
we call the soul.
The excitement in her was contagious.
Karen had a way of making everyone around her
feel enormously alive.

History

History is terrifying

History is terrifying.
All that stuff people do
to each other,
not to mention
the enormous energy and time
it takes to cross the steppes.
And what about that
bunch of strangers
hanging out at the bar?
Looking for trouble, I'd say,
but that's just a guess.
For all we know
they think the trouble
comes from this direction,
and who knows?
They could be right.
The thing about history
is that even when
you know what happens
you never know
the end.

The world keeps getting less

The world keeps getting less real
this summer. Oil in the gulf,
floods in Pakistan, droughts in Africa,
wars all over the place.
Business as usual.
Probably global warming
has something to do with it
but what's the difference?
Nothing's going to stop it,
we know that already.
Treaties, negotiations, petitions,
volunteers, appeals for
this, that, and the other.
More than any other phrase, I detest
give me a break,
but right now I would like to use it.
Listen: even the best of systems
becomes too complex in the long run.
Oh, parts of it can make out okay
for a century or two, sometimes even longer,
but eventually everybody gets tired and dissatisfied.
Life's too hard or too boring or both,
so let's have a revolution or a war.
Better yet one of them followed by the other.
One good result: we'll have great stories to tell,
heroism and tragedy for centuries,
millennia if you are really lucky.
Sure, two hundred or four hundred years from now

some wise guy (or gal) will come along
and say your stories are full of it.
Whatever it was, it didn't happen
the way you wrote it down.
Now her or his new version is the new truth,
and everyone will believe it for a while.
She or he will also have
a much clearer idea of what happened to you
than you ever will.
That, my friend, is history.

There comes a time

There comes a time when you don't want
to think about history any longer.
Not that you can ignore it. Not by a long shot.
It's part of every breath you take this century
and the last, the one full of horrors you can never forget
any more than you can forget the pain in your big toe.
Gout is at best humorous.
It makes you think of Major Hoople,
foot wrapped in a white bandage, propped on a stool,
but who else these days can remember that odd
one-panel cartoon in the Montreal *Gazette?*
You get used to the pain after a while,
the way you get used to history.
It's part of you, like it or not (mostly you don't).
At 74 you have learned the world is the world
and there's not much you can do about it,
not with all the aches you have acquired over the years.
The question remains: could you ever? And did you try?
Less, I suppose, than you like to think or say.
Some speeches against Nixon and the war.
Hey, did you hear the local deli has a new sandwich
named after the president? Baloney on white!
Words like that were fine for a crowd of students
hardly more than a decade younger than you.
Our great contribution to history
was at least half theater, maybe more.
The reason I don't want to think history any longer
is not just because I am becoming history now, sort of.

I see that every day when I shave.
Whose face is that?
Not that I remember the earlier versions.
I never did like looking in the mirror,
though sometimes I would try to convince myself
that what I saw wasn't so bad.
This is the age of wisdom
when you turn to people like Hegel for advice.
Let me confess: I have never before
been able to understand him,
directly or dialectically,
but I do find the introduction
to *The Philosophy of History* right on:
What experience and history teach is this:
that people and governments never
have learned anything from history.
I mean you'd think there is at least one
really clear lesson from the past:
Never invade Afghanistan. Never.
Ask Alexander the Great
who had to marry an Afghan princess
(not such a bad fate)
and pay off a hundred tribal leaders
to make his passage to India.
Ask the Brits, or the Russians.
They know, but we Americans don't trust the past.
We're all students of Herman's Hermits.
Do you remember their big hit?
Don't know much about history
It came out in 1966, the year I started teaching,
long before I knew how smart Hegel was.

29

What is it?

What is it
I've been trying to give them
all these years
in the classroom.
Not history.
that was just a vehicle for something
I would call
self-righteousness,
a moral critique,
but you'd think me pretentious
and so would I
(we are not so different
you know).
It was never just about
wars and revolutions
out of the past
but the ones taking place
in our minds.
Call it a question with no answer
a test of who
we wished to become
and never could.
The rest was details
and theories about
what they mean.
Rising, falling, vanishing,
that's about it for the past.
Almost half a century it took me
to learn people like details

more than theories.
Have you noticed?
True or false,
it doesn't matter much.
You can't help wonder
how will the future
look back on us?
History might come in handy here.
Think of the Romans
not yon Cassius and Brutus
and that whole crew,
but earlier,
maybe a century or so
when someone
must have sensed
some slight change
and then
not so slight
in the language of politics
or the social order.
Which one doesn't matter,
they go together.
Words about corruption
at the highest levels,
the enormous gap between
rich and poor.
Lots of bread and
violent games
to keep the plebs distracted.
Men hurled to the lions,
or was it Bengal tigers?
The times they were a' changin',
the times they had a' changed.

History on Film

Why do we want to know how others felt?
Why do we want their stories from the past?
It always was this way, pretty much, wasn't it?
The clothing was different, the gestures, the accents.
Different noses too, depending where depending when.
How is the real question. How do we
make the days more interesting than our own
spent talking to brilliant kids who can't understand
the seven plus decades you are
laying down for eyes and ears.

Way back in the Fifties
we were not just listening to sh-booom, sh-booom.
There was something else, something more sacred
than the lessons they tossed over our head
like the salads in Sunday School.
When the Jewish People Was Young.
The title offended me. It offends me still.
I wanted to shout at the rabbi,
but you couldn't shout
at someone with a number on his arm.
Change that single word and I might have been
one of those kids who used to
go off to Israel for the summer
and come back so full of stories about the glories
of life on a kibbutz that went on and on for so long
that once you found yourself saying:
So why the fuck didn't you stay there?

The words shocked a room full of relatives,
but they too were tired of hearing endless tales
of planting orange trees in the desert,
floating on the water of the Dead Sea,
dancing the hora round a campfire every night.
He went on to be a famous neurosurgeon, the story teller.
Remember the photo at the Kennedy Center.
Lights. Camera. Action. He's in a tux
and the flash of the bulbs gleams off his teeth.
President Johnson stands right next to him,
or is it Nixon? Either way,
there's a lot of history in that photo
which just might end up in a textbook about
the glorious years of the Diaspora.

This is not poetry

This is not poetry, not the real thing
(though I hope someone or other will think it is)
This is just a historian far beyond a certain age
wondering how he ever got into this racket.
I think it was the morality,
the thought that something big is on your side.
But who? God hasn't spoken directly to me.
Heaven forbid! He certainly hasn't said
anything like: Good Boy! Keep it up!
Even if agents and publishers
turn a cold shoulder to your prose,
I like it and I'm God!
Sometimes I think he speaks through my words,
the ones he must give me because I can't imagine
who else might be on the job.
I can hear the echoes of my mother's voice
in the parts where tears come to my eyes.
The irony is from my father, but it's really
an immigrant voice trying out a new language.
Aristotle drew a sharp distinction
between poetry and history
the first being more important
because what could happen is always more interesting
(and less painful) than what did.

Hollywood

I've never had any illusions about the town
since we moved here when I was in the sixth grade.
A close friend in school was the son
of one of the Hollywood Ten,
and in my family we knew what that meant –
Joe McCarthy, the HUAC, blacklists.
Still, I have liked movies ever since the days
of the Saturday matinee –
three serials, eight cartoons, two features.
Buck Rogers, Hopalong Cassidy.
We rooted for the guys with
blond hair and white skin,
and never cared much about the girls
until a young starlet nobody remembers
moved into a house
just down the block at Fifth and Orlando.
It was right there in the
Sunday Supplement of the *LA Times*.
Not the address, but a photo.
We guys knew the house,
and began to walk past it a lot,
pretending we were on errands,
dutiful boys, helping with the chores,
peeking out the corner of our eyes
but never catching a glimpse.
Once we did see her mother
who wasn't half bad herself
for a woman in her forties,
 elderly, like our moms,

except none of them
lounged in the front garden
wearing a one piece bathing suit.
In the paper the daughter looked pretty.
She hadn't had a speaking role
in a feature film, not yet, but
that didn't matter to us.
We knew the *Times* was right.
She was a regular girl,
sweet, innocent, caring,
a good student too,
liked math and literature and history
though she didn't go to
Fairfax High with us.
One Saturday evening,
as the sun was going down
we were winding up a game,
football or baseball,
I can't remember which
but I do know we were arguing
as usual
over a ball, foul or fair,
in or out of bounds,
when this huge black limo,
a Caddy in those days
when Mercedes still suggested
SS officers on the prowl,
pulled up in front of her house.
A driver in a uniform and cap
got out and went to the door.
We stopped talking and stood
still as pillars of salt when,

wearing a white dress and silver shoes,
her dark hair glittering in
the glow of the street lamps,
Deborah Paget
came out the door,
floated across the yard,
stepped into the limo
and rode off towards immortality.

Cliches and variations

Life is a game,
winners and losers,
referees, coaches,
spectators.
In a glass walled room
high above the field
men spend the afternoon
yelling into microphones.
Cameramen, photographers.
All ages
all colors
all walks of life.
Flags.
Hot dog stands.
Public Restrooms.
Some guys exit whistling,
others slouch away
hands in pockets.
It's a mess out there.
Corruption, payoffs to cops,
rogue priests.
You name it,
we got it
and then some.
Cheerleaders. Clowns. Attorneys.
Historians!
They'll explain it all to us
but it will be too late.

One day (for N on our wedding)

One day your face appeared in a swimming pool.
One day you reached out to me under a tree
full of spring blossoms.
One day in a hotel room
our bodies began to speak a language
our souls already understood.
We knew each other long before the hotel room,
the tree, the swimming pool.
The little girl who dyed her hair blonde
and wore sunglasses to high school in Kabul
jumped into a YMCA pool high above the Pacific
just in time to come face to face
with the little boy from Montreal
whose grandfather swam the Pruth River.
Your face doesn't belong here –
the words came out of my mouth
unbidden. You took offense,
but it was only the startle of recognition.
I remembered your eyes from somewhere
along the Silk Road.
You were the daughter of the Great Khan,
I, a minstrel, composing songs I claimed were true.
There were no swimming pools in that realm.
Your father sent you to an uncle in far off Persia.
My songs grew sad.
I stopped singing and moved to the New World.
Seeing you after all these centuries
makes me want to sing again.

Number the days

You like to number the days.
Every time you say they are counted
I have to wonder if they are already in a book
and if so, one written by whom?
Okay. I joke, but only a little.
As always your look suggests
I am playing some ancient Hebrew game
or passing on an obscure bit of rabbinic wisdom
that somehow made it past the iron gates
of my father's atheism.
I wonder what he and your father
would have had to say to each other
had they ever chanced to meet.
Imagine them face to face
in the climax of one of those Westerns
we both saw in our youth,
you at the Cinema Zeinab in Sharinow,
that part of Kabul bombed to smithereens
by us, or them. Does it matter?
Me at the Picfair Theater on Pico Boulevard,
torn down years ago to make way
for a parking lot.
It is Saturday afternoon
after the two serials, eight cartoons
one huge box of popcorn and a pack of jujubes.
The sun is setting in black and white.
The shadow of their Stetsons
falls across the sharp line
down the center of a dusty street

dividing dark from light.
Two men stride forward
and stop, face to face.
Salaam Aleikam, says your father.
Mine answers: *Shabat shalom*.

Fifty years from now

Fifty years from now our house will be a monument.
I do hope the mattress will have been replaced by then.
I wouldn't want all those tourists
to witness the indentations of our love.

A hundred years from now there will be
monuments all over the world --
Cairo, Bogotá, Kyoto, Salvador de Bahia,
and the capital of Swaziland
even if I can't remember its name.
Mbambane perhaps.
All these places, you and I on a pedestal,
larger than life.

Five hundred years from now our first meeting
will be the stuff of legend, your line
I am a Muslim and will always be a Muslim
repeated by girls around the globe,
part of a chorus in that most famous of operas:
They Met in the YMCA Swimming Pool.

A thousand years from now
we will live again
as we did a thousand years ago
this time in another galaxy
where suffering and pain are forbidden
by order of your father, the Emir.

You and I

You and I, we come and go,
in one world today,
another one tomorrow.
We know who we are but not exactly why.
Y? A crooked letter,
that's what we used to call it.
We were afraid to answer what it asked,
and certainly never thought of asking ourselves.
What if there were no answers?
The truth is I would not have gotten
this far without you.
Not that I can tell exactly where we are,
But I know it's infinitely
more welcoming than any of the other realms
I wandered into over the last seven decades.
Earlier than that, it's pretty much a mystery,
but what matters now is you are here!
If you weren't, I wouldn't even know
there were questions to ask,
let alone the possibility of answers.

On her veins

In her veins
runs the blood of emirs.
Kings are killers, I would say,
like all rulers of countries,
large and small.
But she'd look back at me
with the eyes and nose of
Abdur Rahman Khan
and I would stop.

She likes the idea of
being my muse,
but would like it better
if my books sold
a lot more copies,
maybe a million.
So would I,
but what can you do
when you feel
someone else is choosing
the topics and the words?

I couldn't have said
anything like that
before the years
she began to sleep
beside me every night.
Call it osmosis!
Call it magic!

I mean it's not like she has me
down on a prayer rug
several times a day.
Nothing like that.
It's just that over the years
it seems more and more
as if the whole business,
I mean all of it,
not just this spinning home to
the greater apes
(and the lesser ones),
but the whole shebang
all the way to the edge,
of the universe,
expanding,
collapsing,
vanishing into a black whole,
or all of the above –
that all this just happened –
amoeba, fish, dinosaurs,
and here we are –
is as difficult to believe
as that an old guy
with a long white beard
tossed it together as
a Christmas present
for the universe.

Author's Note
and Biography

Author's Note

The poems in this collection—with the exception of *One Day*, written for Nahid on our wedding day—poured into my consciousness during my mid-seventies when I was contemplating retirement. That is a moment of transition, a time of life when it seems important to come to grips with the infinity we call God. The themes of the poems—laments for vanished times; critiques of my own life and the world, and the relation between the two, past and present; questions about what it is to be a historian in a culture that rushes so quickly to erase the past; celebrations of the unexpected love that has brightened my life in the last two decades—reflect my conscious and unconscious states of mind more consistently and directly than anything else I have written in my more than five decades as an author. I hope they will resonate with readers, old and young, who already have, or soon enough will, live through the daunting changes that modern culture imposes upon successive generations.

Biography

Robert A Rosenstone, a Professor of History at the California Institute of Technology for fifty years, has published fifteen books, including works of biography, history, criticism, and fiction. He has won three Fulbright fellowships, four from the National Endowment for the Humanities, and has been a Fellow at the Getty Research Institute and the East-West Center in Honolulu. Rosenstone has served as a visiting faculty member at the University of St. Andrews, the European University Institute in Florence, the University of Barcelona, Manchester University, Kyushu University in Japan, Tolima University in Colombia, and UCLA. His writings have been translated into eleven languages. *Do People Look Up at the Moon Anymore*? is his first book of poetry. He lives in Pacific Palisades, California with his wife, the photographer, orchid and succulent-grower, and chef extraordinaire, Nahid Massoud.

Details on his career and published works can be found on the website www.rosenstone.com.

Made in the USA
Charleston, SC
07 April 2015